AQUARIUS HOROSCOPE & ASTROLOGY 2025

Mystic Cat

Suite 41906, 3/2237 Gold Coast HWY

Mermaid Beach, Queensland, 4218

Australia

islandauthor@hotmail.com

Copyright © 2024 by Mystic Cat

Time set to Coordinated Universal Time Zone (UT±0)

All rights reserved. This book or any portion thereof may not be reproduced or used in any manner without the publisher's express written permission except for the use of brief quotations in a book review.

The information accessible from this book is for informational purposes only. None of the data should be regarded as a promise of benefits. It should not be considered a statutory warranty or a guarantee of results achievable.

Images are used under license from Fotosearch & Dreamstime.

Contents

January	16
February	24
March	32
April	40
May	48
June	56
July	64
August	72
September	80
October	88
November	96
December	104

Hello there,

Let me explain why my horoscope books may give different readings for each zodiac sign. The sky is always bustling with astrological activity, and I want to focus on what's most important for each star sign.

Every zodiac sign is unique, and the planets up above affect them differently. When I create horoscopes, I pay extra attention to the most critical astrological events for a specific sign. Some days, there might be lots of stuff happening in the stars, but one thing stands out as the essential factor for a particular zodiac sign.

I also consider which planet rules a sign and its associated element. This in-depth consideration helps me tailor my interpretations to match a sign's characteristics.

Ultimately, my goal is to provide you with unique advice and insights that match the cosmic influences for your sign. By focusing on what makes each sign special, I hope to help you understand yourself better and navigate the energies around you. Embracing your sign's strengths and challenges is the key to making my horoscopes feel uniquely aligned for you.

Cosmic Blessings,

Sia Sands

AQUARIUS 2025 HOROSCOPE & ASTROLOGY

Four Weeks Per Month

Week 1 – Days 1 - 7

Week 2 – Days 8 - 14

Week 3 – Days 15 - 21

Week 4 – Days 22 – Month-end

AQUARIUS

AQUARIUS

Aquarius Dates: January 20th to February 18th

Zodiac Symbol: Water Bearer

Element: Air

Planets: Saturn, Uranus

House: Eleventh

Color: Electric Blue

Aquarius is the eleventh astrological sign in the zodiac and belongs to the Air element. Individuals born under the Aquarius sign are known for their innovative, humanitarian, and independent nature. The symbol of Aquarius, the Water Bearer, represents the sharing of knowledge and the flow of ideas.

Aquarius individuals are characterized by their intellectual curiosity, open-mindedness, and desire to bring positive change to the world. They often possess a unique perspective and are drawn to unconventional ideas. Ruled by Uranus, the planet of innovation and sudden change, Aquarians have a strong sense of individuality and a willingness to challenge the status quo.

Aquarius is in the Eleventh House of the zodiac and is associated with friendship, community, and humanitarian pursuits. This placement emphasizes Aquarius' focus on collaboration, social causes, and their desire to make a difference on a larger scale.

Electric blue is often linked to Aquarius due to its connections with innovation, originality, and intellectual stimulation. This color reflects the inventive and forward-thinking qualities of Aquarius individuals.

In summary, Aquarius embodies innovation, humanitarianism, and independence. Those born under this sign often wish to contribute to society's betterment and explore new ideas. Their ability to think outside the box and their dedication to causes make them valuable advocates for positive change.

The Chinese Zodiac is a system that assigns an animal sign to each year in a 12-year cycle, and each animal is associated with certain personality traits and characteristics.

The Year of the Snake, in particular, holds special significance within Chinese culture and is rich in symbolism.

2025

The Chinese Year of the Snake

Aquarians are known for their innovative thinking, intellectual curiosity, and humanitarian outlook. They possess a unique perspective on the world and often seek to make a positive impact through their ideas and actions. When the Year of the Snake arrives, it introduces a blend of energies that can resonate with and challenge the Aquarius personality.

During this year, Aquarians might find themselves drawn to the Snake's qualities of communication and intuition. Just as snakes communicate through various means, Aquarians could enhance their ability to share their visionary ideas effectively with others.

The Year of the Snake encourages Aquarians to explore their intellectual pursuits more deeply. It's a time for them to delve into their passions, uncovering innovative solutions and insights that align with their visionary nature, much like the Snake's ability to navigate its environment precisely.

Aquarius' humanitarian ideals align well with the Snake's adaptability. This year might inspire Aquarians to find new ways to champion their causes, adapting their strategies to create a positive impact and fostering positive change.

The Year of the Snake could encourage Aquarians to connect more profoundly in relationships. Just as snakes rely on their senses to navigate their surroundings, Aquarians might seek to understand the emotions and motivations of those around them, building more meaningful connections.

While Aquarians are known for their originality, the Year of the Snake invites them to explore their inner landscape even more. It doesn't mean sacrificing their individuality; instead, it's about combining their innovative thinking with a deeper understanding of their emotions and motivations.

Ultimately, the Year of the Snake offers Aquarians an opportunity for personal growth and expanded influence. By tapping into the Snake's symbolism of shedding the old and embracing the new, Aquarians can refine their communication skills, foster deeper connections, and continue positively impacting the world while connecting with their inner selves.

AQUARIUS 2025 HOROSCOPE & ASTROLOGY

JANUARY WEEK ONE

☽ As the Moon gracefully moves into Capricorn, you'll sense a significant shift in your emotional landscape. Capricorn's energy imparts discipline and ambition to your feelings, akin to a cosmic CEO taking charge. It urges you to set goals and get down to business, making you more focused on your long-term plans and ambitions. Tackling challenges with determination becomes second nature. Use this time to channel your emotions into productive endeavors and embrace the responsibility that Capricorn brings.

● This New Moon invites you to set intentions, particularly in your career and public image. Whether you're eyeing a new job, embarking on a significant project, or simply seeking a fresh, professional outlook, this is your cosmic reset button. So, grab your dreams and make a wish because the universe is listening and poised to support your journey to the stars.

🌒 As the Moon shifts into Aquarius, prepare for a move toward independence and innovation in your emotional landscape. Aquarius' energy encourages you to break from the norm.

JANUARY WEEK ONE

Brace yourself for a celestial serenade as Venus waltzes into the ethereal realm of Pisces. This cosmic entrance sets the stage for a romantic odyssey.

Fasten your cosmic seat belts for a tempestuous tango that unfolds as Mars and Pluto lock horns in a celestial duel. It's a clash of titans, a battle where desires and transformations meet in a tumultuous dance.

The Moon's graceful drift into Pisces invites you to embark on an emotional odyssey. Pisces beckons you to trust your inner compass, guiding you through your soul's mysteries.

As the Sun forms a harmonious sextile with Saturn, the cosmic stage is set for a symphony of achievement and structure. This celestial alignment grants you the wisdom to build your dreams on a foundation of endurance and excellence.

Prepare for a refreshing cosmic shift as the Moon enters Aries, igniting your inner fire. With the fearless spirit of a warrior, you charge forward, ready to conquer challenges and blaze trails through new territories.

JANUARY WEEK TWO

☀ With Mercury gracefully gliding into Capricorn, the cosmic stage is set for more practical and goal-oriented communication. Your thoughts now gravitate towards long-term plans. Your mind dons a strategist's cap, helping you make well-thought-out decisions and communicate with a clear, business-minded tone.

☽ The Moon's whimsical move into Gemini has you craving intellectual stimulation and social interaction. Your curiosity is piqued, making it a perfect time to engage in lively conversations, explore new ideas, and soak up information like a sponge.

☽ Later, as the Moon glides into Cancer, emotions take center stage. You'll feel a profound connection to home and family, like a cozy embrace from the universe. This lunar transit invites you to replenish your emotional well-being.

● The harmonious trine between Mars and Neptune adds a touch of enchantment to your actions and ambitions. Your energy is infused with inspiration and guided by intuition.

JANUARY WEEK TWO

⚡ The Sun's trine with Uranus electrifies your life with excitement and a thirst for change. You're open to new experiences and receptive to unconventional ideas. It's as if the cosmic winds of innovation are at your back, encouraging you to embrace personal growth and explore uncharted territories.

🌕 The Full Moon, that luminous celestial climax, shines a radiant spotlight on your accomplishments and aspirations. It's a time of culmination, where you can stand in the lunar glow and celebrate your achievements. Simultaneously, it's an opportune moment to reevaluate your goals and make necessary course corrections under the Moon's wise guidance.

🌙 As the Moon makes its grand entrance into fiery Leo, you'll find yourself yearning for the limelight. Your inner performer takes center stage, and you're drawn to activities that allow you to showcase your unique talents.

✦ Venus square Jupiter adds a dash of indulgence to your cosmic cocktail. There's a heightened desire for pleasure and luxury during this aspect.

JANUARY WEEK THREE

☀ When the Sun opposes Mars, cosmic forces create a push-pull dynamic within you. Your desires and actions are in a celestial tug of war. This aspect can bring about increased assertiveness and a passion to assert your will, but it's crucial to temper this energy with patience and diplomacy.

🌙 As the Moon gracefully moves into meticulous Virgo, you'll find yourself in an analytical and detail-oriented mindset. This transit is an excellent time for tasks requiring precision and organization, as you'll have a keen eye for spotting imperfections and improving.

⚡ The Sun's harmonious sextile with Neptune infuses your life with a touch of magic and intuition. You'll find it easier to connect with your dreams and tap into your creative flow. This cosmic alignment encourages you to explore your artistic and spiritual side.

💜 Venus dances into a conjunct with Saturn, creating a blend of love and responsibility. It's like a cosmic commitment ceremony where your relationships take on a more serious tone. This aspect encourages you to evaluate connections and determine their potential.

JANUARY WEEK THREE

As the Moon transitions into balanced Libra, you'll crave harmony and seek out the company of others. Libra's energy encourages cooperation and fairness, making it an excellent time for finding common ground.

Mercury forms harmonious sextiles with Saturn and Venus, enhancing your communication skills and diplomatic finesse. This cosmic duo empowers you to express your thoughts and feelings clearly and tactfully, making navigating complex discussions easier.

The Sun's ingress into Aquarius marks a shift towards innovation and a desire for intellectual pursuits. You'll feel open to unconventional ideas, making it a great time to embrace your inner vision.

The Sun's conjunction with Pluto adds intensity and transformation to your life. It's like a cosmic phoenix rising from the ashes, inviting you to release old patterns and embrace your power.

As the Moon dives into passionate Scorpio, your emotions take on a more profound and reflective tone. Scorpio's energy encourages you to delve into the depths of your psyche and explore hidden truths.

JANUARY WEEK FOUR

💡 Mercury trine Uranus: This aspect sparks brilliant insights and innovative thinking. Your mind is open to unconventional ideas and solutions, making it a fertile ground for creative endeavors and intellectual breakthroughs.

🌙 The Moon's journey into Sagittarius amplifies your thirst for knowledge and adventure. You'll yearn for new experiences and a broader perspective, making it an ideal time for travel or exploring new cultures.

💜 Venus trine Mars: Love and passion harmoniously align in your life during this period. Your romantic and social interactions are infused with charm and desire, creating an atmosphere of warmth and connection.

🌙 As the Moon moves into structured Capricorn, you'll feel the urge to focus on responsibilities and long-term goals. This lunar phase emphasizes discipline and determination.

💬 Mercury sextile Neptune: Your mind becomes a canvas for creative and imaginative thinking. This cosmic alignment encourages artistic and spiritual pursuits, allowing you to express yourself gracefully.

JANUARY WEEK FOUR

☀ Mercury's ingress into Aquarius shifts your thought patterns, making you more open to innovative and progressive ideas. Your communication style becomes more community-oriented.

☽ The Moon's presence in Aquarius aligns with your desire for humanitarian causes and group activities.

● The New Moon marks a fresh start and a blank canvas for setting intentions. It's an ideal time to plant the seeds of your desires and embark on a new journey.

♅ Uranus turns direct, signaling a shift in the energy of change and innovation. You'll find it easier to implement the transformations you've been contemplating.

☽ The Moon's move into Pisces enhances your intuition and emotional sensitivity. You'll be drawn to artistic and spiritual pursuits, seeking solace in the ethereal realms.

☉ Sun trine Jupiter expands your horizons and brings a sense of abundance. Opportunities for growth and optimism abound during this favorable alignment.

FEBRUARY WEEK ONE

💜 When Venus, the planet of love and beauty, aligns harmoniously with dreamy Neptune, matters of love and romance take on an otherworldly, almost ethereal quality. It's as if you're under a love spell, encouraging you to embrace your inner poet and express your deepest affections. This alignment fosters a profound connection to your emotions, allowing you to navigate the seas of love with sensitivity and grace.

🌙 The Moon's entrance into fiery Aries sets your emotions ablaze with passion and assertiveness. You'll feel dynamic energy coursing through you, igniting a desire to initiate new projects and boldly take on challenges head-on. It's a cosmic pep talk urging you to harness your warrior spirit and fearlessly pursue goals.

💬 Mercury's harmonious trine with expansive Jupiter is a celestial megaphone for your thoughts and ideas. Your mental faculties are at their peak, and your intellectual pursuits are infused with boundless optimism and wisdom. This alignment inspires engaging conversations where your words resonate with insight and positivity, making it an ideal time to share your knowledge and seek new horizons.

FEBRUARY WEEK ONE

🐏 With Venus's grand entrance into bold and independent Aries, a burst of fiery energy envelops your love life and personal style. This celestial transition encourages you to embrace desires with confidence.

⏩ Jupiter's direct motion signals a significant shift in the cosmic landscape, marking a period of forward momentum and personal growth. Plans and projects that may have been on hold can now proceed with renewed vigor, and you'll find that the universe opens doors to opportunities for expansion and learning.

🌙 The Moon's journey into chatty and curious Gemini sets the stage for lively social interactions and intellectual exploration. Your communication skills shine brightly, and you'll relish exchanging ideas and engaging in spirited conversations.

💖 Venus's harmonious sextile with transformative Pluto adds depth and intensity to your relationships and desires. This powerful and passionate energy encourages you to explore the profound depths of your emotional connections, fostering a transformative and empowering experience in matters of the heart.

FEBRUARY WEEK TWO

☽ As the Moon gracefully moves into nurturing Cancer, your emotions take on a compassionate and protective tone. It's like a cosmic embrace, encouraging you to prioritize self-care and connect with loved ones on a deeper emotional level. Home and family become central themes during this lunar phase.

☉ The Sun's conjunction with Mercury illuminates your mind with clarity and sharp thinking. Your words flow effortlessly, and you can express your thoughts with precision. It's a favorable time for clear communication and effective decision-making.

♦ Mars' trine with Saturn infuses your actions with discipline and determination. This cosmic alliance empowers you to tackle tasks and projects methodically and efficiently, making it an ideal period for accomplishing your goals.

☽ As the Moon enters vibrant Leo, your emotions are infused with confidence and a desire for self-expression. You'll seek opportunities to shine and showcase your unique talents.

FEBRUARY WEEK TWO

⚡ The Sun's square with Uranus sparks a sense of unpredictability and a craving for change. The cosmos encourages you to break free from routine and embrace your individuality. However, be mindful of impulsive actions during this period.

◐ The Full Moon illuminates the skies, symbolizing a culmination and a turning point in your life. It's a time to celebrate your achievements and, simultaneously, to release what no longer serves your highest good.

☽ As the Moon moves into practical Virgo, your emotions are grounded and detail-oriented. You'll find satisfaction in organization and productivity, making it an excellent time to tackle tasks that require attention to detail.

♥ On Valentine's Day, Mercury transitions into imaginative Pisces, infusing your communications with empathy and intuition. Your compassionate and poetic conversations make it a beautiful time for expressing love and romantic sentiments. Creativity and emotional connection are heightened during this celestial shift, making it a perfect time to celebrate love.

FEBRUARY WEEK THREE

☽ The Moon's gentle entrance into graceful Libra invites you to navigate your emotions with a delicate sense of balance and harmony. During this lunar phase, your heart seeks equilibrium in your relationships and surroundings. You'll find beauty in fairness and may be inspired to create more aesthetically pleasing environments. It is when you'll want to foster peace and understanding in your interactions, valuing cooperation and diplomacy. It's a time when the gentle cadence of your feelings harmonizes with the world around you, encouraging you to seek fairness and equilibrium in your interactions and surroundings.

☽ As the Moon delves deeper into the enigmatic waters of Scorpio, your emotions take on a profound and reflective tone. It's as if a veil is lifted, allowing you to explore the hidden aspects of life and your psyche. Trust your intuition during this phase; it can be a powerful guide. Emotional authenticity becomes paramount, and you may be drawn to transformative experiences that bring growth and healing.

FEBRUARY WEEK THREE

◯ With the Sun's graceful transition into compassionate Pisces, you're entering a period of heightened sensitivity and artistic inspiration. This celestial shift encourages you to embrace empathy and imagination. You'll feel more attuned to the collective consciousness, making it an excellent time for creative endeavors, spiritual pursuits, and acts of compassion. Your intuition becomes a guiding light, helping you navigate the subtle realms of existence.

☽ The Moon's journey into adventurous Sagittarius sparks a sense of optimism and wanderlust within you. You'll crave new experiences, philosophical insights, and the freedom to explore uncharted territories physically and mentally. This lunar phase encourages you to broaden your horizons and embrace the spirit of adventure. You may find inspiration in travel, higher education, or profound philosophical discussions.

◯ Mercury's square with expansive Jupiter creates a vibrant cosmic conversation between your mind and the universe. This aspect infuses enthusiasm and a thirst for knowledge; maintaining practicality is essential. Balancing boundless thinking with realism is crucial.

FEBRUARY WEEK FOUR

☽ As the Moon gracefully enters Capricorn, your emotional landscape takes on a more disciplined and structured tone. This lunar phase encourages you to embrace responsibility and a sense of purpose. You'll find comfort in setting realistic goals and working diligently to achieve them. The Moon in Capricorn also supports your ambitions and offers emotional stability, making it an excellent time for long-term planning and pursuing your aspirations.

⬤ Mars, having completed its retrograde journey, triumphantly turns direct, infusing your actions with newfound vigor and determination. You'll feel a surge of forward momentum and a stronger drive to pursue your goals and desires. This direct motion of Mars empowers you to overcome obstacles and move steadily toward your objectives. The cosmic winds are at your back, propelling you with passion and resolve.

☽ Later, as the Moon transitions into the forward-thinking realm of Aquarius, your emotions take on a more open and progressive quality. This lunar phase encourages you to embrace your uniqueness and seek innovative solutions.

FEBRUARY WEEK FOUR

◌ Mercury's conjunction with Saturn marks a period of focused and deliberate thinking. Your mind becomes a structured and systematic machine, allowing you to approach your responsibilities and tasks precisely. This cosmic alignment supports in-depth, strategic planning and problem-solving. While your thoughts may take on a more serious tone, this aspect grants you the mental discipline and organizational skills needed to tackle even the most complex challenges.

◌ Mercury's sextile with innovative Uranus infuses your thoughts and conversations with brilliance and originality. Your mind is open to new ideas and unconventional solutions during this harmonious aspect. It's a great time to think outside the box and embrace unique perspectives.

● The New Moon marks a fresh beginning in your cosmic journey. It's a time for setting intentions and planting seeds for endeavors. Use this lunar phase to initiate projects, start afresh, and set clear preferences for what you wish to manifest. The energy of the New Moon supports fresh starts and the pursuit of dreams.

MARCH WEEK ONE

🌙 As the Moon swiftly moves into dynamic Aries, your emotions are ignited with passionate and assertive energy. You'll find yourself drawn to action and adventure, eager to take on challenges and confidently lead. This lunar phase encourages you to trust your instincts and embrace your inner warrior.

🪐 Venus, the planet of love and beauty, embarks on a retrograde journey, prompting you to reevaluate matters of the heart and your values. During this introspective phase, you may reflect on past relationships, redefine your concept of love, and explore the depths of your desires. It's a time to seek inner harmony and rediscover what truly matters to you in love and aesthetics.

💬 Mercury's conjunction with dreamy Neptune opens the doors to heightened imagination and sensitivity. Your thoughts and communication take on a poetic and artistic quality, allowing for creative expression and spiritual insights. This cosmic connection encourages you to listen to your intuition and communicate with empathy and compassion.

MARCH WEEK ONE

Mercury's ingress into Aries brings assertive and direct communication. Your thoughts are quick, and you're unafraid to express your opinions confidently. It's a time to initiate meaningful conversations and take action in your mental pursuits.

The Moon's transition into sensual Taurus creates a desire for comfort and stability. You'll enjoy simple pleasures, from delicious cuisine to connecting with nature. Emotionally, this phase emphasizes security and a connection to the physical world.

Mercury's sextile with transformative Pluto adds depth and intensity to your communication and thought processes. This celestial connection encourages you to delve fearlessly into profound subjects and explore the intricate layers of your thoughts. It's a transformative phase for conversations and mental exploration.

The Moon's transition into nurturing Cancer highlights the importance of emotional connection and family bonds. You'll find solace in the comforts of home and may be inclined to promote and support those you love.

MARCH WEEK TWO

☀ When the Sun forms a harmonious trine with Mars, you're infused with a dynamic and confident energy. It's as if the universe gives you a cosmic green light to pursue your goals and assert your desires with vigor.

🌙 As the Moon gracefully moves into radiant Leo, you'll feel the urge to express your individuality and take center stage. Your emotions are colorful and passionate, and you'll seek activities that allow you to shine and share your creativity with the world. It's a time to let your inner performer shine.

💬 Mercury's conjunction with Venus adds a touch of charm and grace to your thoughts and communications. Your words are poetic, making it a perfect time for heartfelt expressions, sweet conversations, and artistic endeavors. This cosmic alignment enhances your ability to connect with others through diplomacy and empathy.

🌙 The Moon's transition into analytical Virgo encourages a focus on detail and practicality. You'll be naturally inclined to pay attention to the finer points of life, seeking perfection in your daily routines and work.

MARCH WEEK TWO

◯ The Sun's conjunction with disciplined Saturn marks a period of increased responsibility and a need for structure. It's a time to assess your long-term goals and make practical plans for the future.

● The Full Moon illuminates your accomplishments and goals, highlighting your achievements. It's a time for celebration and reevaluation, ensuring your ambitions align with your desires. This lunar phase invites you to release what no longer serves you and make space for new aspirations.

⚡ The Sun's sextile with Uranus adds a touch of excitement and innovation. While it can lead to sudden changes or unexpected events, it's also an opportunity to break free from limitations and embrace individuality. This aspect encourages you to welcome the unexpected with open arms and explore new horizons.

☽ As the Moon enters the harmonious sign of Libra, you'll seek balance and harmony in your emotions and relationships. It's a time when you'll be naturally drawn to create peace and fairness in your interactions, prioritizing cooperation and diplomacy.

MARCH WEEK THREE

☉ When Mercury turns retrograde, it's as if the cosmic messenger takes a step back to review and reflect on the past. During this period, you may encounter delays and miscommunications. It's an ideal time to revisit and reassess your plans, tying up loose ends and making necessary adjustments.

☽ The Moon's transition into intense Scorpio brings your emotions to the depths of introspection and transformation. You'll feel a strong urge to uncover hidden truths and explore the mysteries of life. It's a time when your intuition is heightened, making it ideal for inner work and deep emotional connections.

♐ As the Moon progresses into adventurous Sagittarius, your emotions take on a spirited and optimistic tone. It's a cosmic call to explore, learn, and embrace new experiences. Your curiosity knows no bounds, and you'll find joy in expanding your horizons and seeking higher truths. The call for adventure is strong, and you may find pleasure in planning future journeys, whether they involve physical travel or mental exploration.

MARCH WEEK THREE

☼ The Sun's conjunction with Neptune adds a touch of dreaminess and intuition to your life. It's a time when your imagination is heightened, and you may find solace in artistic and spiritual pursuits. This cosmic alignment encourages compassion, empathy, and a connection to the mystical realms.

♈ The Sun's transition into Aries marks the Vernal Equinox, symbolizing the beginning of a new astrological year. It's a time of renewal, where the energy is fresh and vibrant. Your enthusiasm and determination are revitalized, making it an ideal period for starting new ventures and pursuing your goals with vigor.

♀ Venus's sextile with Pluto adds depth and intensity to your relationships and desires. During this cosmic connection, you may experience profound transformations in heart matters. It's a time when you're drawn to passionate and meaningful connections, and your interactions carry a magnetic allure. Embrace the power of love and transformation in your personal life. It's a time for self-reflection and an immersive exploration of your desires while welcoming the transformative power of deep connections.

MARCH WEEK FOUR

🌙 As the Moon gracefully transitions into Capricorn, your emotions take on a more practical and grounded quality. You'll find yourself naturally inclined towards responsibilities and long-term goals. During this lunar phase, the cosmic spotlight is on your duties, and you'll feel ambition driving you to achieve your objectives.

♣ The celestial alignment of the Sun and Venus ushers heightened romance and harmony in your life. It's as if the universe is orchestrating a love symphony, making your interactions brim with affection and beauty. This phase is ideal for expressing your feelings and basking in the finer aspects of life.

✦ The Sun's harmonious sextile with Pluto adds depth and intensity to your experiences. This cosmic connection encourages transformation and empowerment. You delve deep into your desires, effect meaningful changes, and emerge wiser.

☻ The conjunction of the Sun and Mercury is akin to a surge of mental clarity and effective communication. Your thoughts are sharp, and your words carry persuasive power.

MARCH WEEK FOUR

💜 The conjunction of Venus and Neptune further amplifies the dreamy and romantic ambiance. It's a period of heightened creativity and an intense desire to experience transcendent love and beauty.

🌗 As the Moon shifts into Aries, you'll feel a surge of energy and assertiveness. It's a cosmic call to action, urging you to take the lead, embrace challenges, and confidently assert your desires.

🌑 The New Moon heralds a fresh beginning and the opportunity to set new intentions. This lunar phase invites you to plant the seeds of your desires and envision the future you wish to create. It's a moment of renewal and a cosmic blank canvas on which to paint your aspirations.

💭 Mercury's move into Pisces enhances your intuition and empathy in communication. Your words become more compassionate and poetic, creating an ideal environment for deep, heartfelt conversations. You'll naturally connect with others on a profound level.

APRIL WEEK ONE

🌙 When the Moon gracefully glides into Gemini, your emotions become more curious and adaptable. It's as if a desire for knowledge and new experiences fuels your heart. During this lunar phase, you may engage in lively conversations, seek mental stimulation, and embrace variety in your emotional landscape.

🏠 As the Moon transitions into Cancer, your emotions turn homeward. Nurturing and comfort become paramount during this phase, and you're drawn to create a cozy, secure space. Connecting with family and loved ones holds a special place in your heart, and sentimental moments take center stage.

☼ The sextile between Saturn and Uranus brings a harmonious blend of tradition and innovation. This cosmic alignment encourages you to find practical ways to implement change and embrace new ideas. It's a time when you can make gradual yet significant progress in your life, combining the stability of the past with the excitement of the future.

💧 Mars's sextile with Uranus ignites your passion and desire for independence.

APRIL WEEK ONE

☼ When the Sun forms a sextile with Jupiter, it's as though the universe is offering you a helping hand in expanding your horizons. This harmonious connection brings opportunities for growth, abundance, and good fortune. It's a time to say "yes" to new experiences.

♥ Venus's trine with Mars adds an air of romance and passion to your relationships. This celestial partnership fosters harmony between the masculine and feminine energies, creating a beautiful synergy between love and desire. Your interactions are filled with affection and sensuality.

● The conjunction of Venus and Saturn sets the stage for a relationship commitment. It's a time when you're willing to work on the foundations of love and strengthen your bonds through patience and dedication. This aspect encourages responsible and mature expressions of affection.

☿ As Mercury turns direct, a cosmic sigh of relief washes over your thought processes. It's as if the gears of your mind, which may have felt rusty during the retrograde period, begin to move again.

APRIL WEEK TWO

✦ When Venus shares a harmonious sextile with Uranus, the universe sprinkles a little stardust into your relationships and aesthetic tastes. This delightful connection infuses your romantic life with an air of excitement and an openness to unconventional expressions of love. You may find yourself attracted to people or things that are refreshingly different or avant-garde. It's a period where your appreciation for beauty takes on a unique and quirky quality, filling your encounters and artistic endeavors with pleasant surprises.

☽ As the Moon graces Virgo with its presence, you become finely attuned to the small details. Practical matters and the need for order take the forefront.

💜 Transitioning into the harmonious sign of Libra, the Moon becomes your cosmic peacemaker. During this phase, you'll strongly desire emotional balance and harmony in your relationships. Your heart seeks fairness, compromise, and connection with others. You're inclined to see the beauty in symmetry and the art of compromise, making it an ideal time to mend any emotional bridges and embrace the aesthetics of unity.

APRIL WEEK TWO

🌕 The Full Moon is like a celestial spotlight illuminating your achievements and intentions. It's a moment of heightened emotions and revelations, a time to celebrate your successes and acknowledge the outcomes of your hard work. You feel a surge of emotions and a need to release what no longer serves you, paving a fresh start.

☿ As Venus resumes direct motion, the energy of love and beauty flows freely once more. This celestial shift renews your relationships and your appreciation for aesthetics. If you've encountered any hiccups or stagnation in matters of the heart or artistic endeavors, these will begin to flow more smoothly. It's a time of increased harmony, where your love life regains its natural rhythm, and your artistic inspirations find their creative spark.

🌑 The Moon's entrance into Scorpio is akin to a deep dive into the ocean of intense emotions and transformation. During this phase, you'll feel a strong pull towards exploring the mysteries of life and delving into profound truths. Your emotional depth and intuition are heightened, guiding you to confront hidden or uncharted emotional territories.

APRIL WEEK THREE

🌀 When Mercury conjoins Neptune, it's as if your mind drifts into the dreamy realms of imagination and intuition. Your thoughts become more attuned to the subtle and mystical, making it an excellent time for creative endeavors and exploring your spiritual side.

🦁 Mars's ingress into Leo infuses your actions with dramatic flair and self-expression. You'll find that your drive and energy align with your desires and passions. It's a time to pursue your goals with confidence and enthusiasm and celebrate your individuality.

♑ As the Moon moves into practical Capricorn, your emotions take on a more grounded and determined tone. This lunar phase encourages you to focus on your long-term goals and responsibilities, making it an excellent time for planning and organization. You'll find satisfaction in achieving tangible results.

☉ The Sun's entrance into Taurus invites you to connect with the Earth's rhythms and savor life's simple pleasures. Your focus may turn towards financial matters, comfort, and enjoying the beauty of the physical realm.

APRIL WEEK THREE

💜 Venus's sextile with Uranus adds a touch of excitement and spontaneity to your relationships and personal values. You may find yourself drawn to unique and unconventional expressions of love and beauty. It's a time for romantic surprises and exploring new aspects.

💬 Mercury's sextile with Pluto deepens your thoughts and communication. This cosmic connection encourages you to delve into profound and transformative conversations. Your ability to research and investigate complex topics is heightened, making it an excellent time for introspection and uncovering hidden truths.

🌬 As the Moon enters Aquarius, your emotions take on an intellectual and innovative quality. This lunar phase encourages you to seek unconventional solutions and embrace your individuality. It's a time when you may be drawn to humanitarian or group-oriented activities.

☀ The Sun's square with Mars ignites your inner fire and assertiveness. It's a cosmic call to action, but it's essential to channel this energy wisely. Finding constructive outlets for your energy is vital during this phase.

APRIL WEEK FOUR

☾ As the Moon moves into Pisces, your emotions take on a dreamy and compassionate quality. You may find solace in artistic or spiritual pursuits and feel more empathetic towards others.

☉ Sun square Pluto intensifies your power and may bring forth deep transformations. This aspect can feel like a cosmic pressure cooker, pushing you to confront hidden issues or power struggles. It's an opportunity to release what no longer serves your personal growth.

♀ Venus conjunct Saturn brings a sense of commitment and seriousness to your relationships. This cosmic alliance encourages you to strengthen your bonds and work on long-term stability in matters of the heart. While it may feel sober, it paves the way for enduring and meaningful connections.

✷ Mars opposed Pluto, creating a potent cosmic clash between the warrior and the underworld. It can be an intense and transformative period where power struggles and conflicts may arise. This aspect calls for careful handling of personal desires and assertiveness, emphasizing the need for constructive action.

APRIL WEEK FOUR

As the Moon enters Taurus, your emotions seek comfort, security, and stability. It's a time when you're drawn to the pleasures of life, from good food to beautiful surroundings. You may need to connect with nature and enjoy the sensual side of existence.

The New Moon marks a fresh beginning, like a cosmic blank canvas for your intentions. This lunar phase is ideal for setting new goals and initiating projects. It's a moment of introspection and planting the seeds for your future. Embrace the sense of possibility that comes with the New Moon.

With the Moon in Gemini, your emotions become more communicative and curious. It's a time when you'll seek mental stimulation and engage in lively conversations. Your adaptability and versatility shine, making it excellent for learning and socializing.

Venus's ingress into Aries infuses your relationships with passion and spontaneity. This period encourages a fiery and adventurous approach to love and creativity. Enjoy the thrill of the chase and the exhilaration of new connections.

MAY WEEK ONE

☾ As the Moon gracefully drifts into Cancer, your emotions become deeply attuned to matters of home, family, and nurturing. You may find comfort in familiar surroundings and seek emotional security through close connections. This lunar phase encourages you to express your feelings and support loved ones.

💕 The conjunction of Venus and Neptune brings a touch of magic to your love life and creative endeavors. It's a cosmic embrace of romantic and artistic inspiration. You may experience dreamy, almost otherworldly connections with loved ones or be drawn to artistic expressions that touch the soul.

🦁 When the Moon enters Leo, your emotions reflect a vibrant, theatrical flair. It's as if you step onto the cosmic stage, ready to shine and express your uniqueness. This lunar phase encourages self-confidence and the pursuit of your creative passions.

♇ Pluto's retrograde motion signals a time of introspection and profound transformation. This cosmic powerhouse encourages you to explore your inner world, confronting issues related to power and control.

MAY WEEK ONE

Mercury sextile Jupiter expands your mind and communication abilities. This harmonious alignment encourages you to explore new ideas, engage in meaningful conversations, and broaden your horizons. It's an excellent time for learning, travel, and philosophical discussions.

As the Moon moves into Virgo, your emotions become practical and detail-oriented. This lunar phase is a great time for tackling tasks that require precision and organization. You may find satisfaction in achieving small, functional goals and attending to the finer details of life.

Venus sextile Pluto adds depth and intensity to your relationships and creative pursuits. A cosmic connection encourages profound emotional connections and transformative artistic expressions. Your desires run deep, and you're willing to explore the hidden aspects of love and creativity. It's a time for nurturing and expressing your emotions, seeking magic and inspiration in your connections and artistic pursuits, and diving deep into the mysteries of life and self.

MAY WEEK TWO

☀ As the Moon gracefully enters Libra, your emotions seek harmony and balance in your surroundings and relationships. Libra, ruled by Venus, encourages you to appreciate beauty and seek peaceful connections. During this lunar phase, you'll find yourself more attuned to the needs and desires of others, making it an ideal time for diplomatic interactions and enhancing your sense of aesthetics.

🌱 Mercury's ingress into Taurus grounds your thoughts and communication in practicality and sensuality. Your mind becomes focused on tangible matters, and you may have a stronger desire to express your ideas through creative or artistic channels. Taurus encourages you to slow down, savor the moment, and savor the beauty in everyday life.

☾ The Moon's passage into Scorpio intensifies your emotions, diving deep into the mysteries of your inner world. Scorpio's influence encourages you to explore your passions, uncover hidden truths, and embrace transformation. This lunar phase may stir strong emotions and a desire for profound, intimate connections.

MAY WEEK TWO

The Full Moon represents a culmination and a time of realization. It's a celestial spotlight on the intentions you set during the New Moon. Your emotions may run high as you see the fruits of your efforts, and you're prompted to release what no longer serves you, making space for new beginnings.

Mercury's square with Pluto adds a touch of intensity to your thoughts and communication. You may discover deep and transformative conversations or uncover hidden information. This aspect encourages you to explore the shadows of your mind but be mindful of power struggles in your interactions.

As the Moon moves into adventurous Sagittarius, your emotions become free-spirited and eager for new experiences. This lunar phase encourages you to seek knowledge, expand your horizons, and embrace a sense of optimism. You may be drawn to travel, education, or philosophical discussions during this time. This lunar phase encourages you to embrace freedom and seek higher knowledge and understanding.

MAY WEEK THREE

As the Moon gracefully enters Capricorn, your emotions focus on ambition, responsibility, and long-term goals. It's a time when you're more inclined to set practical objectives and work diligently to achieve them. This lunar phase encourages discipline, leadership, and a strong sense of duty. This lunar phase enables you to take a structured approach to your feelings and provides an opportunity for emotional maturity.

When the Sun forms a conjunction with Uranus, it's like a cosmic bolt of lightning, awakening your desire for freedom and change. This aspect can bring unexpected events and innovative ideas into your life. You may feel an urge to break free from routines and embrace individuality.

Mercury's square with Mars creates an atmosphere of mental tension and assertiveness. You might engage in debates, but be cautious of impulsive reactions and hasty decisions. This aspect encourages you to think before you act and channel your energy into productive pursuits.

MAY WEEK THREE

✺ As the Moon moves into Aquarius, your emotions take on a unique and unconventional quality. You're drawn to innovation, social causes, and intellectual pursuits. This lunar phase encourages you to connect with like-minded individuals and explore uncharted territory.

☉ When the Sun forms a sextile with Saturn, it's like a cosmic nod of approval for your hard work and dedication. This aspect brings a sense of stability and a feeling of accomplishment. You may find it easier to establish routines and make responsible decisions.

☾ The Moon's transition into Pisces infuses your emotions with sensitivity and compassion. It's a time when you're more attuned to the intangible aspects of life, such as dreams, intuition, and the arts. This lunar phase encourages a connection to your spiritual self.

☼ With the Sun's move into Gemini, your focus shifts to communication, curiosity, and versatility. It is a time of increased mental activity and a desire to learn and connect with others. You may find yourself embracing a more lighthearted and adaptable approach to life.

MAY WEEK FOUR

💚 Venus trine Mars creates a harmonious dance of love and desire. Your relationships and creative endeavors are infused with passion and a sense of balance. This aspect encourages you to express your affections with grace and embrace the pleasures of life.

☀ The Sun's sextile with Neptune brings a touch of magic to your life. It's as if your intuition and imagination are in perfect harmony, allowing for creative inspiration and spiritual insights. This aspect encourages you to embrace your dreams and pursue your artistic visions.

🔺 Sun trine Pluto marks a period of powerful transformation. You have the strength and determination to make profound changes in your life. This aspect encourages you to embrace your power and work towards your goals with unwavering focus.

♄ Saturn's ingress into Aries is a significant cosmic shift. It's a time when you're called to take a more assertive and independent approach to your responsibilities and goals. This transit encourages self-discipline and taking charge of your destiny.

MAY WEEK FOUR

Mercury's move into Gemini infuses your communication with versatility and curiosity. You're eager to explore a variety of topics and engage in lively conversations. This transit encourages mental agility, learning, and networking.

Mercury's sextile with Saturn enhances your concentration and organizational skills. It's a favorable time for detailed work and structured thinking. This aspect encourages you to make practical and well-thought-out plans.

The New Moon marks a fresh beginning and an opportunity to set new intentions.

Mercury's trine with Pluto intensifies your mental processes and communication. You have a deep and transformative understanding of the subjects that interest you. This aspect encourages profound conversations and a thirst for knowledge.

The Sun's conjunction with Mercury illuminates your thoughts and communication. This aspect encourages clear and impactful expression.

JUNE WEEK ONE

🌿 When the Moon gracefully enters Virgo, your emotions adopt a practical and detail-oriented focus. You're inclined to pay attention to the finer points of life, seeking order and precision in your daily routines. This lunar phase encourages you to nurture a sense of efficiency and take care of practical matters. It's an excellent time to tend to health-related concerns.

⚖ As the Moon moves into Libra, your emotions take on a harmonious and pleasant tone. You're naturally drawn to seek balance and fairness in your interactions with others. This lunar phase encourages cooperation, diplomacy, and the desire to create harmonious relationships. It's a favorable time for socializing and enhancing your connections.

☾ Venus sextile Jupiter forms a delightful connection between love and abundance. Your relationships and personal enjoyment are infused with positivity and optimism. It's a time when you can expand your affections and indulge in life's pleasures, fostering a sense of joy and generosity.

JUNE WEEK ONE

✏ Mercury sextile Mars ignites your mental processes with energy and enthusiasm. Your thinking becomes dynamic and assertive, making it an excellent time for initiating projects and pursuing your goals. This aspect encourages effective communication and the ability to convey your ideas with confidence.

🌷 Venus's move into Taurus brings a sensual and earthy quality to your relationships and values. You're inclined to seek comfort, stability, and physical pleasures in your connections. This transit encourages a deeper appreciation of beauty, as well as a desire to nurture and build security in your love life and finances.

☾ When the Moon delves into Scorpio, your emotions take on a deep quality. You may find yourself drawn to explore the mysteries of life and the hidden aspects of your psyche. This lunar phase encourages self-reflection, transformation, and a desire to delve into profound emotional experiences. It's a time of emotional depth and passion. This lunar phase encourages introspection, emotional healing, and a willingness to confront the truth.

JUNE WEEK TWO

✳ Mercury's conjunction with Jupiter ignites your mind with expansive and optimistic thinking. Your ideas and conversations take on a grand scale, and you're drawn to explore new horizons. This aspect encourages learning, travel, and the pursuit of wisdom.

♋ Mercury's move into Cancer brings a more emotional and nurturing tone to your communication. You'll find yourself expressing your thoughts with empathy and sensitivity, especially in matters related to home and family. This transit encourages heartfelt conversations and a focus on emotional connections.

◻ Mercury's square with Saturn adds a touch of practicality and discipline to your mental processes. You may encounter challenges that require careful planning and attention to detail in your communication. This aspect encourages responsibility and a structured approach to problem-solving.

♐ As the Moon gracefully enters Sagittarius, your emotions take on an adventurous and open-minded quality. You're drawn to explore new experiences, philosophies, and cultures.

JUNE WEEK TWO

🪦 Venus square Pluto can bring intensity and power struggles to your relationships. You may face issues related to control and possessiveness. It's essential to be mindful of power dynamics and work on finding balance and transformation in your partnerships.

🏠 Jupiter's ingress into Cancer marks a shift in the cosmic landscape, bringing expansion and growth to matters related to home, family, and nurturing. This transit encourages emotional fulfillment, expanding your support system, and connecting with your roots.

🌕 The Full Moon is a time of culmination and fruition. It's like a cosmic spotlight illuminating the results of your efforts and intentions. This lunar phase encourages you to acknowledge your achievements and release what no longer serves you, paving the way for new beginnings.

💕 Mercury's sextile with Venus enhances your ability to express love and appreciation through words and gestures. Your conversations become more harmonious and charming, making it an excellent time for connecting with loved ones and fostering cooperative relationships.

JUNE WEEK THREE

⚡ Mars square Uranus brings a surge of erratic and rebellious energy. It's like a cosmic lightning bolt that disrupts the status quo. This aspect encourages you to expect the unexpected, but it also warns against impulsive actions. Channel this electric energy into constructive changes and avoid unnecessary risks.

🌑 Jupiter square Saturn presents a cosmic tug-of-war between expansion and restriction. While Jupiter encourages growth and optimism, Saturn represents discipline and responsibility. This aspect asks you to find a balance between these forces to achieve your goals and make progress without overextending yourself.

☾ As the Moon enters Pisces, your emotions take on a dreamy and intuitive quality. It's like a cosmic lullaby encouraging introspection and a connection to the mystical realms. This lunar phase is ideal for creative and spiritual pursuits and provides a respite from the demands of the external world.

♍ Mars's move into Virgo infuses your actions with precision. This transit encourages you to tackle practical matters and health-related activities with diligence.

JUNE WEEK THREE

◊ As the Moon enters Aries, your emotions become more assertive and self-focused. It's like a cosmic call to action, urging you to pursue your desires and take initiative. This lunar phase empowers you to start new endeavors and assert your individuality.

▨ Jupiter square Neptune creates a tension between your ideals and reality. While Jupiter fuels your dreams and spiritual pursuits, Neptune can cast an illusory veil over the truth. This aspect encourages you to stay grounded while pursuing your visions, avoiding overindulgence or deception.

❦ As the Moon enters Taurus, your emotions gravitate toward stability and comfort. This lunar phase encourages you to connect with the material world, indulge in creature comforts, and appreciate nature.

☼ With the Sun's ingress into Cancer, you enter a new astrological season as it marks the June Solstice, a time of nurturing and emotional connection. Cancer encourages you to focus on home, family, and inner life. It's a season for tending to your emotional well-being and strengthening bonds with loved ones.

JUNE WEEK FOUR

⚡ Mars sextile Jupiter infuses your actions with an abundance of energy and enthusiasm. It's like a cosmic green light, encouraging you to pursue goals with confidence and vigor. This aspect is favorable for tackling challenges and expanding horizons.

🌑 When the Sun squares Saturn, it's as if a cosmic reality check reminds you of your responsibilities and limitations. This aspect can bring feelings of restriction and obstacles, but it also encourages you to approach your tasks with discipline and perseverance, ultimately leading to personal growth.

🌙 The Sun's square with Neptune creates a dreamy and potentially confusing energy. It's like a cosmic fog that can cloud your perceptions and make it challenging to distinguish between reality and illusion. This aspect encourages you to be cautious in your decision-making and seek clarity in your pursuits.

🍃 The Sun's conjunction with Jupiter marks a moment of expansive and optimistic energy. It's like a cosmic blessing that amplifies your confidence and sense of abundance. This aspect encourages you to aim high.

JUNE WEEK FOUR

🌑 The New Moon is a time of fresh beginnings and setting intentions. It's like a cosmic blank canvas, inviting you to plant the seeds of your desires and start anew. This lunar phase encourages you to focus on your goals, release what no longer serves you, and align with your innermost wishes.

🚀 Mercury sextile Uranus adds a touch of innovation and mental agility to your communication. It's like a cosmic spark that inspires creative thinking and original ideas. This aspect encourages you to embrace change, experiment with new concepts, and express your individuality in your conversations.

💧 Sun sextile Mars fuels your actions with motivation and assertiveness. It's like a cosmic energy boost, encouraging you to pursue your goals with enthusiasm and determination. This aspect is favorable for taking the initiative, competing, and tackling challenges.

🦁 Mercury's ingress into Leo brings a more expressive and bold style to your communication. You'll feel confident in expressing your thoughts. This transit encourages you to be charismatic in your interactions.

JULY WEEK ONE

☽ Venus conjunct Uranus brings an element of surprise and excitement to your love life and personal relationships. It's a cosmic spark that ignites a sense of adventure and a desire for new experiences. This aspect encourages you to embrace change and seek out unconventional connections.

♊ Venus's move into Gemini brings a more communicative and curious approach to love and beauty. This transit encourages you to express your affection through words and to appreciate the diversity in your relationships and surroundings.

☾ Neptune's retrograde motion encourages a deeper dive into your dreams, intuition, and spiritual pursuits. It's like a cosmic call to revisit your inner world and clarify your visions. This period encourages introspection, meditation, and inner exploration.

♎ Venus's sextile with Saturn adds a sense of stability and commitment to your relationships and artistic pursuits. This aspect encourages you to build lasting and meaningful connections.

JULY WEEK ONE

♀ Venus's sextile with Neptune enhances your sense of romance, creativity, and idealism. It's a cosmic wave of inspiration that infuses your relationships and artistic endeavors with a touch of magic. This aspect encourages you to express your love and creativity with a dreamy and compassionate flair.

♐ As the Moon enters Sagittarius, your emotions take on a more adventurous and expansive quality. It's like a cosmic journey that fuels your enthusiasm for new experiences and learning. This lunar phase encourages exploration and a desire to broaden your horizons.

Uranus's move into Gemini marks a significant astrological event. It's like a cosmic shift that brings innovation and a fresh perspective to communication and thought processes. This transit encourages intellectual exploration, adaptability, and a willingness to embrace new ideas and technologies.

Venus trine Pluto deepens your emotional connections and brings a sense of transformation to your relationships and creative endeavors. This aspect fosters meaningful connections.

JULY WEEK TWO

☽ When the Moon gracefully transitions into Capricorn, your emotional world takes on a more structured and pragmatic tone. You'll find that your focus shifts towards your long-term goals, career aspirations, and the practical aspects of life. This lunar influence encourages you to embrace your ambitions and approach your emotions with a sense of duty, making it an ideal time for planning and setting clear objectives.

● The Full Moon is a celestial spectacle, marking a point of culmination and release in your emotional journey. It's as if the universe turns on a spotlight, illuminating your achievements and feelings. This phase urges you to reflect upon your recent endeavors and acknowledge your successes. It's also a potent time for letting go of any emotional baggage or habits that hinder your progress. Like a chapter in a book coming to a close, the Full Moon signals the need for closure and the readiness to embrace the next phase of your life.

☽ As the Moon transitions into the airy realm of Aquarius, your emotional landscape gains an innovative and independent flavor. It's a cosmic breath of fresh air, encouraging you to break free from the routine.

JULY WEEK TWO

Saturn's retrograde journey is akin to a cosmic pause button, as the taskmaster of the zodiac initiates a period of introspection and review. During this time, you're prompted to assess the structures and responsibilities in your life. It's as if Saturn, the celestial teacher, wants you to revisit your long-term goals and ensure they align with your authentic desires and ambitions. While retrogrades may bring challenges, they also present opportunities for growth and realignment. Saturn's retrograde invites you to reflect on your commitment to your path and make necessary adjustments.

The Moon's voyage into the ethereal waters of Pisces ushers in a dreamy and compassionate atmosphere. It's as if a cosmic artist takes a brush to your emotions, infusing them with vivid and imaginative colors. This lunar phase encourages introspection, empathy, and a deep connection to your inner world. You may find that your intuition is heightened, and you're more in tune with the emotions of others. It's a time for creative exploration and spiritual contemplation as you navigate the vast ocean of your feelings and embrace the mysteries of the human soul.

JULY WEEK THREE

🌙 As the Moon strides into Aries, the cosmos gifts you with a surge of dynamic energy. It's akin to a cosmic starter pistol, urging you to sprint into action with newfound vigor and passion. Your emotions are ignited, propelling you to embrace your adventurous side and take the reins of your life. During this lunar phase, don't be surprised if you feel an intense desire to pursue your ambitions with fiery enthusiasm, setting the stage for exciting endeavors.

🔄 When Mercury turns retrograde, the celestial messenger of the zodiac initiates a reflective and recalibrating period in the realm of communication and thought. It's like the universe hands you a magnifying glass to scrutinize your ideas, words, and connections. This cosmic event encourages you to pause, rewind, and replay past conversations and situations, offering an opportunity to resolve misunderstandings and fine-tune your thought processes. As Mercury appears to travel backward through the sky, embrace the chance to review, reconsider, and realign your mental landscape.

JULY WEEK THREE

♥ Mercury sextile Venus weaves a harmonious cosmic connection between your mind and heart. It's as if your thoughts and emotions engage in a graceful waltz, creating a symphony of sweet and meaningful communication. This aspect encourages you to express your feelings with eloquence and sincerity, fostering heartfelt conversations and strengthening your connections with others. The universe blesses you with the gift of resonant expression, making it an ideal period for deepening bonds and engaging in tender, affectionate exchanges.

☾ With the Moon's shift into Gemini, your emotions take on a curious and communicative flair. It's as if a cosmic storyteller awakens within you, inspiring a desire to share your thoughts, feelings, and ideas with the world. During this lunar phase, intellectual curiosity blooms, and your communicative spirit thrives. Engage in lively conversations, explore a wide range of topics, and embrace the joy of connection through words. The universe encourages you to be the vibrant and inquisitive social butterfly you are at heart.

JULY WEEK FOUR

🌞 As the radiant Sun enters Leo, it's like a cosmic spotlight shining on your inner performer. Leo, the zodiac's proud and theatrical sign, encourages you to embrace your creativity, confidence, and charisma. This solar ingress fuels your desire to express yourself authentically and bask in the limelight. It's your time to let your unique qualities shine, captivating those around you with your warmth and magnetism.

⚡ When the Sun forms a harmonious sextile with Uranus, you're in for a dynamic cosmic jolt. This planetary alignment infuses your life with a dose of excitement and innovation. It's like a burst of lightning in the night, inspiring you to embrace change and explore new horizons. Your creative thinking and adventurous spirit are ignited, making it an excellent time to step outside your comfort zone.

💔 Venus square Mars introduces a celestial tension between love and desire. It's like a cosmic tango, where the energies of attraction and passion collide. This aspect may bring moments of romantic friction, as your lusts and affections don't always align. Use this time to explore the complexities of your relationships.

JULY WEEK FOUR

● The arrival of the New Moon represents a fresh cosmic beginning. It's a new canvas awaiting your dreams. This lunar phase encourages you to set new goals, start projects, and plant the seeds of your desires.

☼ Sun opposed Pluto ushers in a period of intense transformation. It's like a cosmic showdown between your ego and the depths of your psyche. This aspect encourages you to confront power struggles and control issues, both within yourself and in your relationships. While it may be challenging, it's an opportunity for profound personal growth and regeneration.

♋ With Venus entering Cancer, your emotions and relationships take center stage. It's like a warm and nurturing embrace, encouraging you to connect on a deeper, more emotional level.

☿ When the Sun forms a conjunction with Mercury, it's like a cosmic conversation between your core self and your mind. This aspect enhances your communication skills and mental clarity, making it an excellent time for self-expression and decision-making.

AUGUST WEEK ONE

💔 When Venus forms a challenging square with Saturn, it's as though the cosmic spotlight shines on the delicate balance between love and responsibility in your life. This celestial dance may create a sense of tension, urging you to confront issues related to commitment, boundaries, and the practical aspects of your relationships. The emotional landscape can feel somewhat restricted, but this aspect provides an opportunity to strengthen your connections by addressing any underlying issues and finding common ground. Remember, enduring love often requires effort and understanding, and during this aspect, you have a chance to fortify the foundations.

🌙 Venus square Neptune introduces an element of dreamy ambiguity to your emotional experiences. It's like navigating through a hazy sea of illusions and fantasies. During this aspect, your perceptions in matters of the heart might be somewhat clouded, and you could find yourself yearning for an idealized version of love. However, it's essential to remain grounded and discerning, as Neptune's influence can lead to misunderstandings or misinterpretations. Trust your intuition, and ensure that your bonds align with reality.

AUGUST WEEK ONE

♐ TheMoon's ingress into Sagittarius brings a refreshing breeze of adventure and exploration to your emotional landscape. You'll feel a natural pull toward expanding your horizons, seeking out new experiences, and embracing a broader perspective. Under this lunar influence, you'll be more open to taking risks and pursuing personal growth.

♑ As the Moon moves into Capricorn, a grounded and pragmatic emotional energy takes center stage. You'll find yourself drawn to your responsibilities and long-term objectives as if a cosmic call to duty echoes in your heart. During this lunar phase, satisfaction comes from accomplishing tasks and making tangible progress in your professional life or personal ambitions. You'll appreciate structure and the sense of achievement that accompanies it.

♎ Mars's ingress into Libra introduces a desire for harmony, balance, and diplomacy. It's as if the cosmic scales tip in favor of cooperation. This shift encourages you to approach conflicts with a graceful demeanor, striving to find equilibrium in your interactions. Your efforts to maintain peace draw balanced foundations.

AUGUST WEEK TWO

🚀 When Mars forms a trine with Uranus, it's like a cosmic ignition switch has been flipped. This aspect blends the bold, action-oriented energy of Mars with the innovative, unconventional spirit of Uranus. You'll feel a surge of motivation and a desire to break free from the ordinary. Expect a burst of creative and inventive energy that propels you forward.

♎ However, the cosmos takes a different turn when Mars opposes Saturn. This celestial face-off pits the fiery, impulsive nature of Mars against the structured, disciplined energy of Saturn. You may find yourself facing challenges, obstacles, or a sense of frustration as you attempt to assert your desires. This aspect urges caution and strategic thinking, emphasizing the importance of planning and patience. While it might slow your progress, it also offers an opportunity to refine your goals and develop a sustainable approach.

🌕 The Full Moon represents a culmination, a moment of illumination and release. This phase amplifies emotions and brings ongoing situations to a climax. It's a time for reflection and evaluation. You'll need to find a balance between your instincts and your rational mind.

AUGUST WEEK TWO

Mars's opposition with Neptune introduces a sense of haziness and confusion to the mix. It's like a fog rolling in, obscuring your path and adding a touch of uncertainty. While Mars pushes you to act, Neptune might encourage you to proceed with care and intuition.

As Mars forms a trine with Pluto, a powerful transformational force comes into play. It's like harnessing the intensity of a storm to bring about change. Mars lends its energy and drive to Pluto's deep transformative qualities, making this a time of great personal empowerment. You'll be determined to overcome obstacles and face any challenges head-on. This aspect encourages you to dig deep, confront your fears, and emerge stronger than before.

When Mercury turns direct, it's as if a communication switch that was on pause is finally back in action. The confusion and miscommunications that may have plagued the retrograde period begin to clear. It's a time for resolving issues, making decisions, and moving forward with plans that may have been on hold. You'll feel a sense of relief as clarity returns to your thinking and communication.

AUGUST WEEK THREE

⚡ When Mercury forms a harmonious sextile with Mars, it's as if the universe aligns your mental prowess and assertive communication in a powerful dance. Your thoughts gain an extra dose of clarity and precision, transforming your words into potent tools for conveying your intentions effectively. This astrological aspect creates a dynamic environment where you excel at planning, problem-solving, and engaging in conversations that leave a mark. It's a time to harness the synergy between your intellect and assertiveness to tackle tasks with precision and enthusiasm.

☽ The Moon's graceful ingress into Gemini opens up the channels of curiosity in your mind. Think of it as an invitation to explore, learn, and adapt. During this lunar phase, you're naturally drawn to new information and fresh ideas. It's an excellent time to dive into stimulating discussions, indulge in reading, or explore diverse subjects. Your mental agility is at its peak, making complex concepts more accessible and learning an enjoyable pursuit.

AUGUST WEEK THREE

✦ The cosmic encore of Mercury's sextile to Mars amplifies your mental acuity and assertiveness. Your capacity to communicate your thoughts with conviction is heightened. It's akin to having a sharp tool in your intellectual toolkit for any problem-solving or planning you need to undertake. This aspect encourages you to be clear, focused, and proactive in your interactions, helping you cut through mental clutter with ease.

☽ As the Moon moves into Cancer, a shift towards the emotional and nurturing aspects of life occurs. This lunar phase is like a warm, comforting embrace from the cosmos. You might feel more attuned to your own emotions and those of the people around you. It's a time when home and family take precedence, and you find solace in creating deep, meaningful connections.

☽ With the Moon gracing Leo, the cosmic stage is set for a more flamboyant and creative expression of your personality. This lunar influence encourages you to shine in the spotlight, embrace your inner artist, and share your unique talents with the world. It's a period where joy, playfulness, and a touch of dramatic flair infuse your daily life.

AUGUST WEEK FOUR

☺ As the Sun enters diligent Virgo, you'll likely feel a shift towards practicality and precision in your life. This solar transit encourages you to pay attention to the details, organize your affairs, and focus on self-improvement. It's a time for setting realistic goals and making steady progress in your endeavors.

☽ The New Moon brings with it a fresh start, making it an excellent time to set new intentions and begin projects with renewed energy. This lunar phase marks a blank canvas where you can paint your dreams and aspirations. Use this time to set clear goals, plant the seeds of your desires, and commit to personal growth.

⚡ The Sun's square to Uranus introduces an element of surprise and change into your life. This aspect can bring unexpected events or revelations that may disrupt your routine. While it may feel unsettling, it's an opportunity to break free from limitations, embrace innovation, and express your individuality.

♥ Venus graces Leo with its presence, infusing your relationships and creative endeavors with warmth and enthusiasm.

AUGUST WEEK FOUR

Venus's trine to Neptune adds a dose of enchantment and creativity to your love life and artistic pursuits. Your emotions are heightened, and your imagination soars, making it a perfect time for creative expression and romantic gestures.

On the flip side, Venus's opposition to Pluto introduces some intensity and power struggles in your relationships. Be mindful of possessiveness and control issues during this period.

The harmonious sextile between Uranus and Neptune opens a doorway to creative and spiritual exploration. It's a time when your intuition is heightened, and you may find innovative ways to connect with your inner self and the world around you.

This week, the celestial influences bring a dynamic mix of energies into your life, offering both opportunities for growth and moments of introspection. Embrace this period as a time of transformation, innovation, and deepening your connections with the world and those you love.

SEPTEMBER WEEK ONE

🍃 Saturn's ingress into Pisces is a significant cosmic event that ushers in a period of deep introspection and emotional exploration. You'll find your focus shifting towards matters of the heart and the soul. This transit encourages you to seek a more profound connection with your inner self and the world around you. It's a time to explore your dreams and nurture your intuition, embracing the power of empathy and compassion.

📓 As Mercury moves into the pragmatic sign of Virgo, your mental faculties receive a boost in precision and detail-oriented thinking. You'll excel in tasks that demand meticulous attention, making this a great time to streamline your life and take a closer look at your health and well-being. Your mind is sharp, and your ability to solve complex problems is heightened.

⚡ When Mercury squares Uranus, brace yourself for a surge of mental energy and potentially unexpected insights. This aspect sparks innovation and creativity, but it can also bring a touch of restlessness. Embrace the spirit of change and remain open to new ideas. It's a time to break free from mental routines and embrace the excitement of the unknown.

SEPTEMBER WEEK ONE

The Mars Jupiter square creates an ambitious and adventurous atmosphere. You'll feel a surge of motivation and desire to expand your horizons. However, be mindful not to take on too much at once, as this aspect can lead to overextending yourself. Pace your efforts, and this energy can lead to remarkable achievements.

Uranus turning retrograde prompts a period of internal reflection and review. It's time to revisit the changes and innovations you've experienced in recent months. Use this phase to integrate newfound insights and seek deeper meaning in your life. Your journey toward liberation takes a more introspective turn during this retrograde.

The Full Moon brings culmination and fulfillment to your recent endeavors. It's a moment to reap the rewards of your hard work and reflect on the intentions you set during the previous New Moon. Emotions may run high, so embrace this time for self-awareness and deep introspection. Embrace the opportunities for growth and self-discovery that this planetary movement offers, and navigate this cosmic dance with grace and wisdom.

SEPTEMBER WEEK TWO

☾ The Moon's ingress into Aries ignites a spark of dynamism and courage in your emotional realm. You're filled with a desire to take action and assert your individuality. It's a fantastic time to initiate new projects, pursue your passions, and embrace a go-getter attitude that propels you forward. The Aries Moon encourages you to take the lead and channel your inner pioneer.

☾ As the Moon transitions into Taurus, a sense of stability and practicality envelops your emotional landscape. During this phase, you'll prioritize comfort and security. It's the perfect time to indulge in life's sensual pleasures, nurture your physical well-being, and focus on financial matters, grounding yourself in the material world.

☉ The Sun's harmonious sextile with Jupiter brings a burst of optimism and opportunity into your life. This cosmic alliance encourages you to broaden your horizons, both mentally and physically. It's an excellent period for setting ambitious goals, exploring new territories, and approaching life's challenges with unwavering confidence.

SEPTEMBER WEEK TWO

With the Moon's entrance into versatile Gemini, your curiosity and sociability are elevated. You're naturally inclined to seek intellectual stimulation, engage in lively conversations, and connect with a diverse range of people. This phase enhances your communication skills and encourages a free exchange of ideas.

Mercury's sextile with Jupiter enhances your communication prowess and intellectual capacities. Your ability to convey ideas effectively is at its peak, making this an ideal time for planning, learning, and sharing your insights with a broader audience. It's a cosmic invitation to expand your mental horizons and explore new intellectual territories.

When the Sun aligns with Mercury in conjunction, your thoughts and self-expression are finely tuned. This celestial union sharpens your intellect and strengthens your communicative powers. It's an auspicious time for vital discussions, making decisions with clarity, and ensuring your voice is heard and understood. Embrace the dynamic interplay of this cosmic force to make the most of the present moment.

SEPTEMBER WEEK THREE

💜 As Venus forms a delightful sextile with Mars, it's like the universe orchestrating a harmonious duet between the planets of love and desire. This cosmic connection can infuse your relationships with an extra dose of romance and passion, making it an ideal time to embrace and express your affections.

💬 However, be prepared for Mercury's opposition with Saturn, which may temporarily throw a communication curveball your way. Conversations might feel weightier, and it can be a bit challenging to convey your thoughts clearly. Take this as an opportunity to practice patience and careful articulation.

✨ With Mercury's graceful ingress into the diplomatic and balanced sign of Libra, you'll find yourself inclined to seek harmony and cooperation in your interactions. It's an ideal period for mending fences, resolving conflicts, and fostering mutual understanding.

🌙 Yet, Mercury's opposition to Neptune may cast a somewhat dreamy and enigmatic hue over your thought processes. It's a time when things might not be as they seem, so be vigilant about potential misunderstandings.

SEPTEMBER WEEK THREE

❀ Venus' entrance into pragmatic Virgo encourages a more meticulous and detail-oriented approach to your love life. You'll find pleasure in tending to the finer aspects of your relationships, whether it's through acts of service or showing your love in practical ways.

⚡ However, the square between Venus and Uranus introduces an element of unpredictability in your relationships. Sudden shifts or unconventional romantic interests could enter your sphere. Embrace the unexpected with curiosity and an open heart.

☼ The Sun's opposition with responsible Saturn may present challenges in the realms of self-expression and personal authority. It's a time when you may encounter obstacles that require patience, discipline, and perseverance to overcome.

● The arrival of a New Moon signifies a fresh beginning, a chance to set intentions and embark on a path of self-discovery and personal growth. Think of it as a cosmic blank canvas where you can paint the next chapter of your life. Navigate this cosmic current with an open heart, a clear mind, and unwavering determination. ✦

SEPTEMBER WEEK FOUR

☼ The September Equinox marks a significant shift as we transition from one season to another. It serves as a celestial reminder to find equilibrium and balance in your life. Just as nature adapts to the changing seasons, you're encouraged to adapt to life's evolving circumstances. Take a moment to reflect, realign your goals, and find the stability you need to navigate the journey ahead.

♎ With the Sun's entrance into Libra, your focus turns to relationships. You're naturally inclined to seek harmony and fairness in all your interactions. This period encourages you to mend any imbalances in your personal and professional connections, fostering a sense of equilibrium and mutual understanding.

⚡ The Sun's trines with Uranus and Pluto infuse your life with transformative and innovative energies. You become more open to change and receptive to new ideas and experiences. This heavenly phase is a period of substantial personal growth, and you'll find that you're more adaptable and resilient than ever.

SEPTEMBER WEEK FOUR

🌙 As the Moon moves into Scorpio, you're drawn into the depths of your emotions and motivations. It's a time for introspection, self-discovery, and understanding the driving forces behind your actions. This emotional journey can lead to profound personal insights and transformation.

🏔 The Moon's subsequent entry into Sagittarius ushers in a sense of adventure and expansion. Your emotions take on a more open and exploratory quality. You're drawn to new horizons, both in your intellectual pursuits and emotional experiences. It's an ideal time to embark on a quest for personal growth and broaden your horizons.

🔺 The Moon's entry into Capricorn shifts your focus to ambition and long-term goals. It's an ideal time for strategic planning and diligent work toward your most significant life objectives. The celestial energies support your efforts to achieve lasting success and take concrete steps toward your dreams. The divine energies support your efforts to achieve ongoing success.

OCTOBER WEEK ONE

🌙 As the Moon glides into Aquarius, a refreshing breeze of individuality sweeps over you. You might find yourself with a newfound urge to break free from the ordinary, eager to embrace your unique self. It is a time to let your intellectual curiosity roam free, explore unconventional ideas, and engage with your community, perhaps even supporting humanitarian causes close to your heart.

🌑 However, with the square aspect between Mercury and Jupiter, there may be a tug-of-war between the nitty-gritty details and grand, expansive thinking. It's essential to balance your optimism with a practical approach, making sure that your lofty ideas can be grounded in reality. Use this cosmic tension as a driving force to finesse your plans.

🌒 Transitioning into Pisces, the Moon imparts an ethereal quality to your emotions. You're likely to feel a heightened sense of empathy and compassion. This period is ideal for reaching out to others, showing kindness, and nurturing your creative or spiritual side. Dive into activities that allow you to explore the depths of your inner world.

OCTOBER WEEK ONE

🚀 With the Moon stepping into Aries, your energy levels soar, and you're primed for action. Embrace your goals with fiery determination and unwavering courage. Whether it's a project, a hobby, or a personal quest, your assertiveness shines through, propelling you forward.

🕵 As Mercury moves into Scorpio, your thinking takes on a more profound and intense tone. You'll be inclined to investigate matters with a magnifying glass, delving deep into complex issues. It is a phase for introspection, where the desire to uncover hidden truths is paramount.

🌕 The Full Moon casts its luminous glow, creating a beacon of illumination. It is a moment of culmination, where intentions set during the New Moon come to fruition. It's also a time for self-reflection and the release of what no longer serves you.

In this cosmic odyssey, the Moon's transitions usher in an array of emotions and activities. Aquarius ignites your individuality, Pisces fosters compassion, and Aries fuels your assertiveness. With Mercury's arrival in Scorpio, your thoughts venture into deeper waters, while the Full Moon brings the culmination of intentions.

OCTOBER WEEK TWO

🌙 As the Moon gracefully enters Taurus, the cosmic energy grounds you in the material world, urging a connection with the tangible and a celebration of life's sensory pleasures. Embrace a slower pace, savor the beauty around you, and let a sense of stability nurture your emotional well-being.

⭐ The harmonious sextile between Venus and expansive Jupiter unfolds a celestial tapestry of warmth and generosity. Relationships take center stage, adorned with grace and kindness.

🌘 Transitioning into Gemini, the Moon encourages intellectual exploration and vibrant communication. Your mind becomes a playground for ideas, sparking lively conversations and stimulating mental curiosity. Engage in discussions, share your thoughts, and let the free exchange of ideas enrich your inner world.

🌓 Venus, now in Libra, engages in a cosmic dance with stern Saturn through opposition. This alignment prompts a delicate balance between desires and practical considerations. Exercise patience and diplomatic finesse to navigate any tension gracefully.

OCTOBER WEEK TWO

💜 Venus, gracing Libra's elegance, encounters an opposition with dreamy Neptune. This aspect introduces a touch of ambiguity to matters of the heart. Exercise discernment and strive for clarity, avoiding idealizations in relationships.

🔄 Pluto's direct motion signals a powerful cosmic shift, encouraging transformative growth and the release of outdated patterns. Embrace this period of inner renewal and let go of what no longer serves your highest purpose.

☀ The Moon's arrival in Leo adds a radiant and theatrical touch to the cosmic stage. Express your authentic self, embracing creativity and self-assurance.

🌙 Venus, in a harmonious trine with innovative Uranus, injects excitement into love and creative pursuits. Embrace spontaneity and openness to unconventional expressions of affection.

🌈 Venus's trine with Pluto deepens the tapestry of passion and intensity in your connections. This cosmic alignment invites transformative experiences in matters of the heart and creative endeavors.

OCTOBER WEEK THREE

☽ As the Moon gracefully enters Virgo, a cosmic call to order and organization echoes in the celestial symphony. It's a time to pay attention to the finer details, refine your routines, and bring a sense of precision to your endeavors—Channel Virgo's diligent and analytical energies to enhance your efficiency and effectiveness in daily pursuits.

☀ A celestial showdown unfolds as the radiant Sun squares expansive Jupiter. This cosmic clash urges you to find a delicate balance between confidence and humility. While Jupiter encourages optimism and growth, the square with the Sun signals a need to ground your aspirations in practicality. Use this cosmic tension as a catalyst for thoughtful expansion and a realistic approach to your goals.

☽ The Moon's transition into Libra brings a touch of grace and harmony to the cosmic stage. Libra, ruled by Venus, invites you to explore the beauty in your surroundings, fostering a sense of balance and cooperation in your relationships. Embrace diplomacy and common ground as you navigate social interactions.

OCTOBER WEEK THREE

🚀 Mercury, the messenger, joins forces with assertive Mars in the cosmic dance of conjunction. This alignment adds a burst of dynamic energy to your communication style. Words become tools for action, and assertiveness can lead to effective outcomes. However, tread with awareness, as the hunger of Mars may intensify discussions.

🌑 The New Moon graces the skies, marking the beginning of a lunar cycle. This celestial reset invites you to set intentions for the upcoming weeks, planting seeds of growth and transformation. Embrace the energy of new beginnings, and let the cosmic canvas be a space for the manifestation of your aspirations. The New Moon marks a potent moment for setting intentions and initiating new cycles in your life. 🌙 ✨

♏ The Moon's ingress into Scorpio invites you to explore the depths of your emotions and unveil hidden truths. Scorpio's energy encourages introspection, transformation, and a willingness to face the shadows within. Dive into the mysteries of your psyche, allowing the lunar glow to illuminate the path of self-discovery.

OCTOBER WEEK FOUR

☀ As the radiant Sun enters the enigmatic realm of Scorpio, transformative energy permeates the cosmic landscape. This solar transit invites you to embrace the depths of your emotions and embark on self-discovery.

🌑 The square between the Sun and Pluto adds a layer of intensity to the celestial narrative. This cosmic dance may bring power dynamics and transformative energies to the forefront. Navigate this potent alignment with a sense of empowerment and a willingness to undergo necessary changes.

✦ The trine between assertive Mars and expansive Jupiter amplifies your drive and enthusiasm. This celestial collaboration fuels your ambitions and provides the energy needed to tackle challenges with confidence. It's a time to set bold goals and take decisive action towards your aspirations.

☾ Mercury's trine with dreamy Neptune adds a touch of enchantment to your mental landscape. This alignment enhances your creativity, intuition, and ability to connect with subtle energies. Allow your imagination to soar and explore the mystical realms of thought.

OCTOBER WEEK FOUR

Mercury's journey into Sagittarius adds a dash of adventure and philosophical exploration to your mental pursuits. Your thoughts may expand beyond the conventional as you seek wisdom, higher knowledge, and a broader perspective on life.

Mars' trine with stabilizing Saturn brings a harmonious dance between action and discipline. This cosmic collaboration provides a structured approach to your endeavors, allowing you to manifest your goals with perseverance and strategic planning.

Mercury's opposition to electrifying Uranus introduces an element of surprise and innovation to your thought processes. Be open to unexpected insights and unconventional ideas, and consider how they can be integrated into your plans.

Mercury's sextile with transformative Pluto adds a depth of insight and analytical prowess to your mental pursuits. This alignment empowers you to delve into the layers of complexity, uncover hidden truths, and engage in profound psychological exploration.

NOVEMBER WEEK ONE

🌙 The Moon gracefully enters Aries, infusing the cosmic atmosphere with a burst of fiery and impulsive energy. Embrace a sense of spontaneity and courage as you navigate the dynamic landscape of your emotions and desires.

💔 Venus squares Jupiter, creating a celestial tension between the planet of love and beauty and the expansive energy of Jupiter. Be cautious of overindulgence and extravagance in matters of the heart and finances. Seek balance and moderation to avoid potential pitfalls.

🚀 Mars forms a harmonious trine with Neptune, blending the assertive and dynamic energy of Mars with the dreamy and imaginative influence of Neptune. This cosmic alliance encourages you to channel your power into creative and spiritual pursuits. Engage in activities that align with your higher aspirations and dreams.

🔥 Mars charges into Sagittarius, igniting a fiery and adventurous spirit within your actions and desires. Embrace a sense of exploration, enthusiasm, and a willingness to take bold initiatives as you embark on new journeys and pursuits.

NOVEMBER WEEK ONE

🌷 The Moon glides into Taurus, bringing a stabilizing and earthy influence to your emotional landscape. Take a moment to ground yourself, appreciate life's simple pleasures, and connect with the beauty of the world.

⚡ Mars opposes Uranus, creating an electric and potentially disruptive energy. Be mindful of impulses and rebellious tendencies. Channel this dynamic force into constructive outlets to avoid unnecessary conflicts and disruptions.

🌕 The Full Moon graces the celestial stage, illuminating the sky with its radiant glow. This cosmic transit marks a culmination of energies, urging you to reflect on achievements, release what no longer serves you, and embrace a sense of completion.

👥 The Moon dances into Gemini, enhancing your communicative and curious nature. Embrace intellectual pursuits, engage in meaningful conversations, and allow your mind to wander into the realms of knowledge and curiosity.

💕 Venus enters Scorpio; dive into your relationship emotions and explore the transformative power of love.

NOVEMBER WEEK TWO

🌀 As Uranus, the cosmic revolutionary, boldly strides into Taurus, the celestial orchestra resonates with the vibrations of change. This cosmic tango promises to reshape the very foundations of your existence, urging you to remain agile and adaptable. The essence of Taurus, associated with stability and material realms, now encounters the electrifying force of Uranus, inviting you to reconsider your relationship with security, possessions, and the earthly domains of life.

💔 The intricate dance between Venus and Pluto unfolds as a cosmic drama that penetrates the profound depths of your relationships. This celestial choreography acts as a cosmic alchemist, compelling you to confront hidden truths and transform challenges into opportunities for growth. In the crucible of Venus square Pluto, relationships undergo a metamorphic process, shedding old layers to reveal a revitalized connection.

🔄 Mercury, the celestial messenger, embarks on its retrograde pilgrimage. As Mercury retraces its steps, it offers an opportunity for introspection, revision, and recalibration. Use this cosmic pause to reassess plans and realign your mental compass.

NOVEMBER WEEK TWO

🐻 Shifting the lunar spotlight to Leo, the cosmic script invites you to become the star of your narrative. This creative phase encourages you to express yourself authentically, unleashing the vibrant hues of your inner artist. Embrace the cosmic applause and let your unique light shine.

🔍 Jupiter, the expansive wanderer, begins its retrograde journey, prompting a reflective pause in the cosmic rhythm. This period invites you to review your beliefs, aspirations, and the grand tapestry of your life's journey. Use this time to fine-tune your philosophy, refine your goals, and align with the expansive wisdom within.

💨 In a dynamic celestial collaboration, Mercury joins forces with Mars, infusing the cosmic narrative with mental vigor and assertiveness. This cosmic duo empowers your communication style, urging you to express your thoughts boldly. However, caution is advised to avoid potential clashes arising from impulsive words and hasty actions. It encourages you to express your thoughts with precision, tackle challenges, and navigate potential conflicts with strategic finesse.

NOVEMBER WEEK THREE

☺ A harmonious trine between the Sun and expansive Jupiter fills your days with optimism and a sense of abundance. This cosmic alliance encourages you to embrace opportunities for growth and explore new horizons. It's a time to shine brightly and radiate positivity in all your endeavors.

☄ Sun's trine with Saturn introduces a stabilizing force into your life. Your efforts align with a sense of discipline and structure, paving the way for long-term success. This cosmic alliance empowers you to build on solid foundations and manifest goals with resilience.

◪ Mercury's sextile with transformative Pluto adds depth to your communication style. Your words carry a profound impact, and your ability to penetrate beneath the surface fosters meaningful connections. Dive into the realms of research and introspection, uncovering hidden truths.

♏ Mercury's ingress into Scorpio deepens your thoughts and sharpens your intuition. Your mind becomes attuned to the mysteries of life, and a desire to explore the unseen motivates your intellectual pursuits.

NOVEMBER WEEK THREE

☾ Mercury's trine with dreamy Neptune adds a touch of magic to your mental landscape. Your imagination flourishes, and creative inspiration flows effortlessly. Engage in artistic endeavors, explore your dreams, and let intuition be your guide.

● The New Moon heralds a fresh beginning, a cosmic reset that invites you to set new intentions and embark on a journey of self-discovery. Take this opportunity to plant seeds for future growth and transformation.

○ The Sun's conjunction with Mercury amplifies your communicative powers. Your mind is sharp, and your ability to articulate thoughts is heightened. It's a favorable time for discussions, negotiations, and expressing yourself with clarity.

♐ Mercury's transition into Sagittarius expands your mental horizons. Your thoughts soar to new heights, seeking wisdom and understanding. Embrace the spirit of adventure in your intellectual pursuits.

♅ Uranus's sextile with Neptune infuses your life with a blend of innovation and imagination. This cosmic dance invites a visionary approach to your endeavors.

NOVEMBER WEEK FOUR

🔗 Grounded wisdom permeates your communication as Mercury forms a harmonious trine with Saturn. Practicality and a long-term perspective infuse your thoughts and words. Utilize this cosmic connection to build solid foundations for your ideas and projects.

📖 An intellectual odyssey unfolds as Mercury engages in a celestial conversation with Jupiter. Open your mind to grand ideas and explore learning or teaching on a broader scale. Positive thinking and an expansive perspective characterize this alignment. Seize the opportunity to communicate with optimism and enthusiasm, embracing the cosmic synergy to explore new concepts.

🌙 Transformational energies abound with the Sun, forming a harmonious sextile with Pluto. Empowerment is the key theme, urging you to tap into your inner strength and instigate positive changes. Resilience becomes your ally, helping you overcome challenges and wield influence over your circumstances. Embrace this cosmic support to delve into personal growth and unlock your potential for positive transformation.

NOVEMBER WEEK FOUR

 Venus and Jupiter unite in a harmonious trine, creating an atmosphere of abundance and joy in matters of love and pleasure. Celebrate the finer things in life, expanding your capacity for love and enjoyment.

 Stability and commitment characterize relationships and creative endeavors as Venus forms a harmonious trine with Saturn. Emphasis is placed on building lasting foundations in matters of the heart and artistic pursuits. Connections deepen, and creative projects gain structure and longevity under this celestial influence.

 Saturn, the cosmic taskmaster, turns direct, signaling progress in areas where you've diligently worked towards your goals. A disciplined and steady approach to your ambitions is encouraged, providing greater clarity and purpose as you move forward.

 Mercury, the cosmic messenger, turns direct, lifting the fog of retrograde energies. Communication flows smoothly, and delays and misunderstandings begin to resolve. Seize the moment to move forward with plans, make decisions, and express your thoughts with increased clarity.

DECEMBER WEEK ONE

☽ As the luminous Moon gracefully steps into the steadfast sign of Taurus, you may feel a grounding influence settling over your emotional landscape. Taurus, an earth sign ruled by Venus, invites you to indulge in sensory pleasures and find comfort in the familiar. This cosmic shift encourages you to savor the simple joys of life, cultivating a sense of stability and security in your emotional world. Take a moment to appreciate the beauty that surrounds you, and allow yourself to be anchored in the serenity of the Taurus energy.

♥ In a celestial dance, the planet of love, Venus, forms a harmonious sextile with powerful Pluto, creating an atmosphere charged with intensity and passion. Your relationships may experience a transformative energy, deepening connections and sparking profound emotional experiences. This cosmic alignment invites you to explore the depths of your desires and embrace the potential for positive change in matters of the heart.

☽ The Moon swiftly glides into the curious and communicative realm of Gemini.

DECEMBER WEEK ONE

The cosmos unveils a spectacle with the arrival of the Full Moon, casting its radiant glow across the night sky. This culmination phase brings a heightened sense of awareness and emotional intensity. It's a time to release what no longer serves you and bask in the illuminating energy of completion. Emotions may run high, so allow yourself to navigate this celestial tide with grace and a spirit of letting go.

Nestled into the nurturing waters of Cancer, the Moon invites you to turn your attention inward and focus on matters of home and family. Cancer's energy is tender, fostering a sense of emotional connection and a desire for comfort and security. Let the Cancer Moon cradle you in its gentle embrace, encouraging emotional replenishment.

A celestial symphony unfolds as communicative Mercury forms a harmonious trine with dreamy Neptune. Your thoughts and words become infused with poetic inspiration and heightened intuition. It's a time for creative and spiritual insights as the boundaries between logic and imagination blur. Allow the current of this cosmic harmony to guide open expression.

DECEMBER WEEK TWO

🜂 The cosmic battlefield witnesses a clash between assertiveness and restraint as Mars squares off against Saturn. It's a celestial call to action, demanding a strategic and measured approach to your ambitions. This cosmic tussle encourages you to build your dreams on a solid foundation, embracing challenges as opportunities for growth.

🌙 As the Moon elegantly glides into meticulous Virgo, your emotional landscape becomes a realm of practicality and precision. Take this time to organize your thoughts, declutter your vibrant space, and bring methodical clarity to your inner world.

🌀 The ethereal realms experience a shift as Neptune turns direct. This celestial movement clears the fog surrounding your dreams and inspirations, unveiling the path forward. Trust your intuitive compass, for it gains newfound reliability.

⚡ Mercury, the quicksilver messenger, engages in a celestial tête-à-tête with rebellious Uranus. Brace yourself for mental fireworks and innovative sparks. Your usual thought patterns might receive a cosmic call.

DECEMBER WEEK TWO

☾ Mercury then forges a harmonious trine with Neptune, blending intellect with inspiration. Your communication style takes on a poetic, compassionate tone, fostering a deep understanding in your interactions.

♐ Mercury boldly ventures into the expansive realms of Sagittarius, widening the horizons of your thoughts. Embrace a spirit of adventure, let your mind wander, and explore the landscapes of curiosity.

♎ The Moon gracefully pirouettes into Libra, casting a soothing balm of balance over your emotional world. Seek harmony in relationships, appreciate the beauty of fairness, and find joy in the equilibrium of give-and-take.

☽ Mercury's harmonious sextile with Pluto adds depth and intensity to your communications. Engage in profound conversations where the power of your words can catalyze transformative change.

☾ However, navigate the cosmic waters with care as Mars squares off against Neptune. Ambitions may encounter illusions or hidden obstacles.

DECEMBER WEEK THREE

♐ As the Moon transitions to Sagittarius, the energy shifts from the profound to the adventurous. Your emotions are infused with a sense of optimism and a desire for exploration. It's a time to broaden your horizons, both emotionally and mentally, as you seek new experiences and perspectives.

🌑 The New Moon marks the beginning of a lunar cycle, a cosmic blank canvas upon which you can set new intentions and sow the seeds of your dreams. Take a moment to reflect on your aspirations and envision the path ahead. Plant the seeds of your desires with the intention of growth and manifestation.

♑ With the December Solstice, the Sun enters Capricorn, marking a pivotal moment in the celestial calendar. It is a time of balance, as daylight and darkness find equilibrium. It also signifies a shift towards grounded and practical energies, urging you to focus on your long-term goals and ambitions.

♑ Mars, the fiery warrior, dons the earthy cloak of Capricorn. Your drive and ambition now take on a structured and disciplined form.

DECEMBER WEEK THREE

😬 However, the Sun's square with Saturn may cast a shadow on your aspirations. Challenges and obstacles may arise, testing your resolve and determination. Approach them with patience and a strategic mindset, for they are stepping stones on your path to achievement.

☾ Sun square Neptune adds a touch of mysticism to the cosmic equation. Navigate the waters of illusion and reality with discernment, ensuring that your dreams are anchored in practicality. Use your intuition as a guiding star, but keep a firm grip on reality.

💔 Venus squares off against Saturn, creating tension in matters of the heart and creativity. It's a call to reassess your commitments and make sure they align with your values. Take a pragmatic approach to relationships and artistic endeavors, ensuring a solid foundation.

♑ With the Sun's ingress into Capricorn, the cosmic spotlight now illuminates themes of responsibility, ambition, and structure. It's a time to set realistic goals and embark on a journey of disciplined achievement.

DECEMBER WEEK FOUR

♥ As Venus embarks on a cosmic dance with Neptune, an enchanting yet potentially intricate energy envelops matters of the heart. The lines between reality and illusion may blur, prompting the need for careful discernment in navigating relationships. It's essential to avoid overly idealizing situations or individuals and strive for clarity in emotional connections.

✦ Venus gracefully transitions into the structured realm of Capricorn, bringing a sense of order and responsibility to expressions of love and appreciation for beauty. During this phase, practical considerations may influence romantic pursuits, encouraging the establishment of solid foundations. Thoughtful gestures of love can be particularly impactful during this period.

☾ The Moon glides into the dreamy waters of Pisces, inviting you to explore the poetic landscapes of emotion and intuition. This celestial alignment heightens sensitivity and compassion, providing an opportune moment for artistic endeavors, meditation, or introspective journeys to connect with your inner self.

DECEMBER WEEK FOUR

 Embark on a cosmic journey as the Moon takes the bold leap into Aries, infusing you with a dynamic surge of initiative and an intense craving for action. Ride the wave of this energetic force, using it to confront challenges and assert your individuality in diverse areas.

 Follow the celestial trail as the Moon transitions into the grounded realms of Taurus. Immerse yourself in the richness of sensory experiences that bring joy to you.

 Witness a celestial drama unfold as Mercury engages in a cosmic tussle with Saturn, creating a delicate dance between communication and structure. Navigate this divine alignment with careful and deliberate expression, acknowledging potential challenges in conveying your ideas. Exercise patience and diligence, using this time to refine your thoughts and concepts.

 Experience the enchanting lunar waltz as the Moon gracefully pirouettes into the inquisitive realms of Gemini. Feel the ignition of intellectual curiosity and a heightened proficiency in communication during this lunar phase. Embrace the chance to explore novel ideas and revel in the adaptable nature that this brings.

NOTES

NOTES

NOTES

Astrology, Tarot & Horoscope Books.

Mystic Cat

www.ingramcontent.com/pod-product-compliance
Lightning Source LLC
LaVergne TN
LVHW051844080426
835512LV00018B/3054